TOMATOES ON TRIAL

The FRUIT v. VEGETABLE Showdown

LINDSAY H. METCALF   Illustrated by **EDWIN FOTHERINGHAM**

CALKINS CREEK

AN IMPRINT OF
ASTRA BOOKS FOR YOUNG READERS
New York

John Nix just wanted a tomato.

Make that a *boatload* of tomatoes. But you can bet your salt, tomatoes don't grow in snow!

The produce king of New York didn't blanch. He had collected cauliflower from California and fruit from Florida. And now in early 1886, he planned to bite into the year's first tomatoes—and get royally rich.

USA

Atlantic
Ocean

NIX & CO

N NIX &

YO

Well-to-do Northerners would pay a pretty penny for the spring's first fruits.

Each year, John Nix & Company forged farther south to live up to the "No. 1" stenciled on their crates.

They had visited Virginia . . .

    convoyed to the Carolinas . . .

        and flocked to Florida.

Competitors caught on. So in spring 1886, Nix and his sons peeled away from the mainland and steamed into the Atlantic.

They found their bounty in Bermuda.

Loaded with green tomatoes, the Nixes' steamship paddled back to the Port of New York, expecting to slide like butter into the United States.

The Customs House collector, Edward Hedden, melted that idea.

"Vegetables," Hedden labeled the tomatoes. Then he slapped them with the 10 percent vegetable tax.

VEGETABLES?!

Nix burned red. These imported morsels were *fruits*!

Fruits the government did not tax like foreign vegetables!

Exhibit one: fruits have seeds (ahem, tomatoes).

Exhibit two: fruits grow from flowers (yep, TOMATOES!).

Too bad the tax collector cared less about botany and more about the law . . .

Exhibit One

Exhibit Two

. . . particularly one law: the Tariff Act of 1883.

After the Civil War, lawmakers wanted the United States to grow strong without help from other countries. So Congress cooked up a grocery list of goods produced in the thirty-eight states. Most items imported from other countries would face taxation if they competed with homegrown goods.

Hedden felt a patriotic duty to whip up jobs at home. Farmers grew fine tomatoes all over the United States every summer. If Nix wanted to haul them in from overseas, he would have to pay up!

1883 IMPORTATION TARIFF ACT

TAXED GOODS

• Vegetables (most)
• Sugar
• Candy
• Chocolate
• Cheese
• Milk
• Molasse

Horseradish! (Speaking of vegetables.)

Nix blew steam. His profits were evaporating with the tax.

But he began to chew on the problem. The word *tomato* did not appear on the tariff list. The tariff law simply said taxes would nip most imported vegetables—not most fruits.

Tomatoes belonged on Team Fruit . . . right?

Hedden stood stiff as celery on Team Vegetable.

Before the precious produce could rot on the water, Nix forked over the tax money.

But he vowed to give Hedden a taste of justice.

The *Nix v. Hedden* case simmered slowly through local and state courts.

The lawsuit even outlived Hedden, who died of pneumonia in February 1893.

After six years of stewing, the case boiled over into the US Supreme Court.

OUR JUDICIARY 1893

UNITED STATES JUDGES

SURROGATES

COURT OF APPEALS

SUPREME COURT OF THE UNITED STATES

Here Lies
EDWARD HEDDEN

CITY COURT OF N.Y.

90 1891 1892 1893

Frank W. Nix

George W. Nix

John W. Nix

John Nix

Edwin B. Smith, Esq.

TEAM FRUIT
PLAINTIFFS

The fruit v. vegetable question was about to be fleshed out in the highest court in the land.

The plaintiffs lined up on Team Fruit.

The defendants faced off on Team Vegetable.

READY? Set...

Elizabeth Hedden

William Arden Maury, Esq.
US Assistant Attorney General

TEAM VEGETABLE
DEFENDANTS

FOOD FIGHT!

Team Fruit fired the first blow: tomatoes have seeds, so the dictionary calls them a fruit. **BOOM!** They slung definition after definition.

FRUIT **$QUISH!**

the produce of a tree or other plant . . .
the seed of plants, or the part that contains the seeds

VEGETABLE **WHOMP!**

such plants as are used for culinary purposes, and cultivated
in gardens, or are destined for feeding cattle and sheep

TOMATO **SPLAT!**

a garden-plant and its FRUIT

Catch up, TEAM
VEGETABLE!

Team Vegetable volleyed back. Fruits may have seeds, but people call some foods with seeds vegetables! They skewered dubious definitions:

PEA

SQUASH

THWACK!

a plant of the genus Cucurbita, and its FRUIT: a culinary vegetable

PLINK!

a plant and its FRUIT, used for food

Can it, TEAM FRUIT!

Team Fruit flipped the recipe.

What makes edibles vegetables? The nutritious roots, leaves, and stems—the plant parts that *don't* contain seeds.

CARROT

POTATO

TURNIP

PARSNIP

ROOT!
a common garden vegetable

ROOT!
a well-known esculent root

ROOT!
a white, esculent root

ROOT!
a garden vegetable or root

CAULIFLOWER

CABBAGE

STEMS!
a species of cabbage

LEAVES!
A garden plant

While the facts marinated, Team Fruit grilled two produce peddlers. The experts agreed the meanings plucked for "fruit" and "vegetable" were true.

The fate of tomatoes lay on the table. Justice Horace Gray dished out the court's unanimous verdict.

VEGETABLE?!

"Affirmed." The court declared people eat tomatoes like vegetables—in main courses instead of desserts.

The decision nixed the Nixes' goal of getting back the tariff money, but . . .

VEGETABLE

FRUIT

. . . spring sprung again, and John Nix & Company returned to work buying and selling produce. Because no matter how you dice the definitions, bellies still relished the fruits—and vegetables—of their labor.

What do YOU think?

While the Supreme Court ruling on tomatoes still stands, tariff laws have changed, so calling tomatoes fruits or vegetables no longer matters much, money-wise.

That means you can judge for yourself! Should tomatoes belong on Team Fruit or Team Vegetable?

How to Debate

John Nix, 1895   Edward Hedden, 1885

The *Nix v. Hedden* case shows us how to use evidence to construct an argument. This is helpful when you want to persuade someone to agree with you.

First, study the topic thoroughly before you form an opinion. Gather evidence from credible sources to support your opinion. Double- and triple-check facts against other credible sources to make sure they are true.

Second, use the facts you found to explain why you believe you are right.

Third, listen to arguments from the other side. Perhaps they will change your mind. If they do, that's OK. If not . . .

Fourth, respond with more evidence that supports your opinion.

To win a debate, research all sides of your topic. Try to understand why your opponent may believe what they believe.

Nix v. Hedden Definitions

The parties in the US Supreme Court case cited definitions from three dictionaries in use or in print in the late 1800s: *Webster*'s dictionary, *Worcester*'s dictionary, and the *Imperial* dictionary. Here are examples of definitions similar to those used in court:

Team Fruit
fruit: "The produce of a tree or other plant . . . the seed of plants, or the part that contains the seeds." (*Webster*'s, 1830)

vegetable: "Such plants as are used for culinary purposes, and cultivated in gardens, or are destined for feeding cattle and sheep." (*Webster*'s, 1830)

tomato: "A garden-plant and its fruit." (*Webster*'s, 1868)

cabbage: "A garden plant." (*Webster*'s, 1868)

carrot: "A common garden vegetable." (*Webster*'s, 1868)

cauliflower: "A species of cabbage." (*Webster*'s, 1868)

parsnip: "A garden vegetable or root." (*Worcester*'s, 1860)

potato: "A well-known esculent [edible] root." (*Webster*'s, 1868)

turnip: "A white, esculent root." (*Worcester*'s, 1860)

Team Vegetable

cucumber: "The name of a plant and its fruit . . . The flower is yellow and bell-shaped, and the stalks are long, slender and trailing on the ground, or climbing by their claspers." (*Webster*'s, 1828)

pea: "A plant and its fruit, used for food." (*Webster*'s, 1868)

pepper: "A plant and its hot, pungent seed." (*Webster*'s, 1868)

squash: "A plant of the genus Cucurbita, and its fruit; a culinary vegetable." (*Webster*'s, 1828)

Today's Definitions

fruit: "The usually edible reproductive body of a seed plant, especially: one having a sweet pulp associated with the seed." Also: "A succulent plant part . . . used chiefly in a dessert or sweet course." (Merriam-Webster.com)

vegetable: "A usually herbaceous plant (such as the cabbage, bean, or potato) grown for an edible part that is usually eaten as part of a meal." (Merriam-Webster.com)

tomato: "The usually large, rounded, edible, pulpy berry of an herb (genus *Solanum*) of the nightshade family native to South America that is typically red but may be yellow, orange, green, or purplish in color and is eaten raw or cooked as a vegetable." (Merriam-Webster.com)

Extra Credit Words

Congress: Consisting of the House of Representatives and the Senate, Congress has the power to make laws. It makes up the legislative branch of the United States government, one of three branches.

defendant: The party being accused in a lawsuit.

import: Something brought into a country from another country.

plaintiff: The person who brings a lawsuit.

Supreme Court: The top court in the United States, which decides whether laws follow the Constitution. Courts make up the judicial branch of government, the second branch. (The third is the executive branch, or the president.)

tariff: A tax on imports.

tax: Money charged by the government.

verdict: A decision in a court case.

US Supreme Court, October 1892 to January 1893. Front row, from left: Horace Gray, Stephen Johnson Field, Chief Justice Melville Fuller, John Marshall Harlan, Samuel Blatchford. Back row: Henry Billings Brown, Lucius Quintus Cincinnatus Lamar, David Josiah Brewer, George Shiras, Jr. In January 1893, four months before the *Nix v. Hedden* case was decided, Lamar died and was replaced by Howell E. Jackson (not pictured).

ESTABLISHED 1839.

JOHN NIX & CO.,

FRUIT AND PRODUCE

Commission Merchants

281 WASHINGTON ST., NEW YORK.

Florida Oranges & Vegetables a Specialty.

Direct Receivers of California Fruits.

HEADQUARTERS FOR BERMUDA PRODUCE.

This Nix advertisement appeared in the Fruit Trade Journal and Produce Record, January 17, 1891.

Author's Note

First off, I'm on Team Vegetable. Tomatoes taste like vegetables! Which is probably why, for most of my life, I didn't like them (gasp).

Raw tomatoes, that is. I was the kid who doused everything in ketchup, and my mom's deep-dish pizza, slathered in red sauce, was my favorite food. It wasn't until adulthood that I tasted in-season, homegrown tomatoes—the kind that glow red all the way through, burst with sweetness, and give no hint of mealiness.

My childhood on a Kansas farm rarely included homegrown tomatoes, surprisingly. My parents must have been too busy tending the vast spreads of wheat, corn, soybeans, and milo (feed grain) to nurture a kitchen garden.

Now that I'm grown, I raise tomatoes in a patch of soil next to my driveway. We transplant seedlings in early May, after the last frost. We water the vines and watch them overtake their cages. And we wait, wait, wait—until the first juicy globes, warm from the summer sun, pop off the vine and into our mouths. Few things are more rewarding.

Whether you side with Team Fruit or Team Vegetable, I hope you will try growing tomatoes wherever you can find a patch—or pot—of soil.
—Lindsay H. Metcalf

Tomato Facts

- By 1879, the United States churned out 19 million cans of tomatoes in a year.
- Today the US makes available about 80 pounds of tomatoes annually for every citizen—the weight of an average newborn rhino.
- In 2011, Congress decided schools could count pizza sauce as a serving of vegetables.
- Tomatoes come in every color of the rainbow, plus black and white.
- The wild ancestor to all tomatoes grows pea-size berries in the South American countries of Peru, Ecuador, and Chile.
- Tomatoes and potatoes are related. The green parts of both are poisonous and called nightshades.
- A few of the early words for tomato: *tomata*; love apple; *xitomatl* (Aztec); and *tomate*, which is still used in Spanish.

Team Fruit Roster

European Union (since 2001)
Ohio (state fruit)
Tennessee (state fruit)
Arkansas (state fruit . . .)

Team Vegetable Roster

United States (since (1893)
New Jersey (state vegetable)
Burpee Seed Company
Arkansas (. . . *and* state vegetable)

Selected Primary Sources

All quotations used in the book can be found in the following sources marked with an asterisk (*).

An act to reduce internal-revenue taxation, and for other purposes, 22 Stat. 488, 47th Congress, 2nd Session, Ch. 121: 488–526, March 3, 1883. fraser.stlouisfed.org/title/tariff-1883-5892.

Buffalo (NY) *Enquirer*. "Obituary (Edward L. Hedden)," February 7, 1893.

Fruit Trade Journal and Produce Record. "Nix Company Celebrates," February 21, 1914.

——. "Virginia Truck Farms," January 20, 1917.

Miami News. "John Nix & Co. Move into New Offices in New York," March 8, 1911.

*United States Supreme Court. *Nix v. Hedden*, 149 U.S. 304 (1893), decided May 10, 1893, tile.loc.gov/storage-services/service/ll/usrep/usrep149/usrep149304/usrep149304.pdf.

*Webster, Noah. *An American Dictionary of the English Language*. New York: S. Converse, 1828 ed., webstersdictionary1828.com.

*Webster, Noah, and Wheeler, William Adolphus. *A Common-school Dictionary of the English Language, Explanatory, Pronouncing, and Synonymous: With an Appendix Containing Various Useful Tables*. United States: J.B. Lippincott, 1868.

*Worcester, Joseph E. *A Comprehensive Dictionary of the English Language*. Boston: Brewer and Tileston, 1860.

Selected Secondary Sources

Smith, Andrew F. *The Tomato in America: Early History, Culture, and Cookery*. Urbana and Chicago: University of Illinois Press, 2001.

Taussig, F. W. *The Tariff History of the United States*, 5th edition. New York and London: G. P. Putnam's Sons, 1910, cdn.mises.org/Tariff%20History%20of%20the%20United%20States_4.pdf.

Online Sources

Estabrook, Barry. "Why Is This Wild, Pea-Sized Tomato So Important?" *Smithsonian* magazine, July 22, 2015. smithsonianmag.com/travel/why-wild-tiny-pimp-tomato-so-important-180955911/.

Merriam-Webster dictionary online. Merriam-Webster.com.

Acknowledgments

Special thanks goes to Andrew F. Smith, author of *The Tomato in America*, for vetting this manuscript; also to Carolyn Yoder, Thalia Leaf, and the delectable Calkins Creek team, who never once flung rotten tomatoes as this book developed.

Picture Credits

Fruit Trade Journal, Dairy and Produce Record, vol. 11–12 (1894–1895): 28 (left), vol. 3–4 (1890–1891): 30; *Frank Leslie's Illustrated Newspaper*, vol. 59–61 (Jan.–Dec. 1885): 28 (right); Library of Congress: LC-USZ6-366: 29.

In memory of Halley Hanson, a fabulous tomato grower and
even better grandma —*LM*

For my family, always —*EF*

Calkins Creek
An imprint of Astra Books for Young Readers,
a division of Astra Publishing House
astrapublishinghouse.com
Printed in China

ISBN: 978-1-6626-8053-3 (hc)
ISBN: 978-1-6626-8054-0 (eBook)
Library of Congress Control Number: 2024941040

First edition

10 9 8 7 6 5 4 3 2 1

Design by Barbara Grzeslo
The text is set in Helvetica Neue.
Display lettering by Edwin Fotheringham
The illustrations are done in blotted line and color wash.